OUR TEDDIES, OURSELVES

OUR TEDDIES, OURSELVES

A Guide to the Well Bear

by

Margaret and Douglas Palau

Illustrated by
Dianne Cassidy

LITTLE, BROWN AND COMPANY

Boston　　　　Toronto

For Nellie

Second Printing

Library of Congress Cataloging in Publication Data

Palau, Douglas.
  Our Teddies, ourselves.

  Summary: A home companion on teddy bear care with
instructions for preparing a first aid kit and for
dealing with squeezles, beary beary, Goldilock's
syndrome, seamitis, and other maladies.
  1. Teddy bears — Anecdotes, facetiae, satire, etc.
[1. Teddy bears — Wit and humor. 2. Toys — Wit and hu-
mor] I. Palau, Margaret. II. Cassidy, Dianne, ill.
III. Title.
PN6231.T673P3 1983   818'.5402   83-11347
ISBN 0-316-68920-3 (pbk.)

                            WOR

*Published simultaneously in Canada
by Little, Brown & Company (Canada) Limited*

PRINTED IN THE UNITED STATES OF AMERICA

EQUIPMENT
AND
SUPPLIES

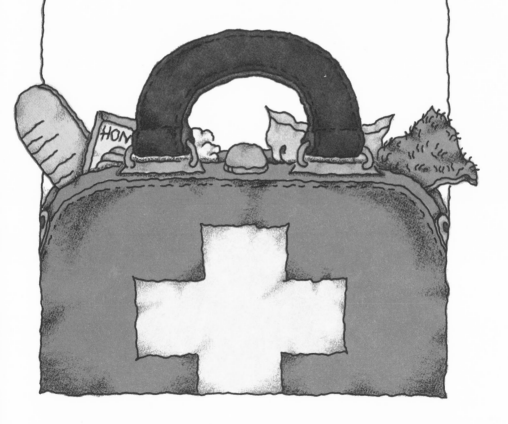

A TEDDY CARE KIT is the first thing you'll need to take care of your Teddy. This is something like a real doctor's bag, but specially made for Teddies. Here are some of the things you should have in it:

 **Eye Buttons** Old buttons that have fallen off shirts, used to make new eyes.

Ambulance A wagon, tricycle, or skateboard, for moving a Teddy too weak to walk.

Bandages Old T-shirts cut into strips and rolled up.

Band-Aids Teddies like them better if you color them to match their fur.

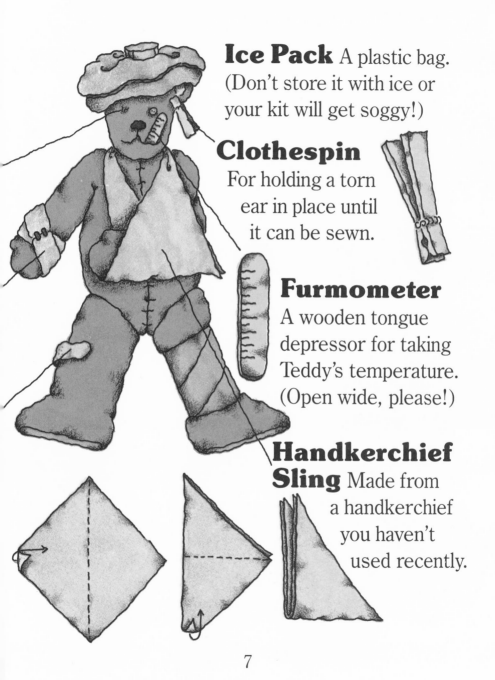

Ice Pack A plastic bag.
(Don't store it with ice or your kit will get soggy!)

Clothespin
For holding a torn
ear in place until
it can be sewn.

Furmometer
A wooden tongue
depressor for taking
Teddy's temperature.
(Open wide, please!)

Handkerchief Sling Made from
a handkerchief
you haven't
used recently.

Honey Packets

For sore throats and for Teddies who have been extra good.

Fur Patch An old piece of fur, felt, or a terry-cloth towel, for those unexpected rips.

Cotton Balls

(Or old, clean nylon stockings.) To make new stuffing.

Tooth Mirror

To check how well Teddy has been brushing.

Paper Towel Roll

For a cast or splint.

TAKING CARE
OF YOUR BEAR

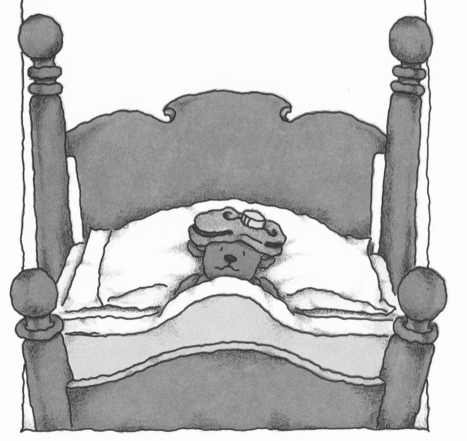

SQUEEZLES

Teddies who have been hugged too tightly will sometimes develop Squeezles. This often happens during thunderstorms, or while reading a beary scary story. The most obvious symptom is a bear who is suddenly much longer than he used to be.

TREATMENT:

Try to squoosh your Teddy back into his original shape. Then wrap him in a bandage and cradle him in your arms. There, he's better already.

BEARY BEARY

If your Teddy's fur feels warmer than it usually does, he may have Beary Beary, or bear's fever. This happens when a Teddy takes an accidental spin in the dryer, or is left in the backseat of a car on a hot summer day.

TREATMENT:

Take your Teddy's temperature using a furmometer. Is he bearly well? Or worse? If his fever is slight, place him in a cool spot and feed him chilled berries. More severe cases may require an ice pack and a little tea — with honey, thank you.

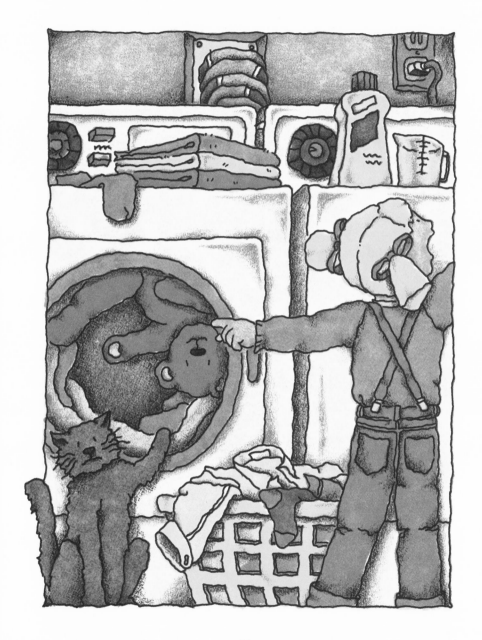

GOLDILOCKS' SYNDROME

A Teddy given too much attention may soon begin to think he's a real boy or girl. If you've noticed half-eaten porridge, a broken chair, or suspect someone has been sleeping in your bed, your Teddy may have this problem.

TREATMENT:

Place your Teddy in front of a mirror and repeat: "You are a Teddy, you are a Teddy." Don't set a place for Teddy at the dinner table for several days. Leave him in his room with a little honey and a copy of *Bears' Life*.

SEAMITIS

Every once in a while, you should check your Teddy over. If you notice that he is coming apart under the arms or along his side, he may have Seamitis. This is quite common in bears handed down by older brothers and sisters.

TREATMENT:

Use cotton balls to replace any lost stuffing. Then sew Teddy together again.

A fur patch will be useful if seams are frayed. Ask your mother or father to help by pleading in a very sad voice: "Hurry, he's bearly breathing!"

WANDERING BEAR

This is a Teddy who can't be found anywhere. Bears with this problem have been known to disappear before picnics, family get-togethers, and even on long car trips. One such bear vanished in a Howard Johnson's in Maryland and was never seen again.

TREATMENT:

At home, try to remember where you were playing with Teddy last. Check that place first. Away from home, make Teddy a tag with his name and address on it. And keep him with you at all times — especially in Maryland.

BEAR'S TOOTHACHE

Many people think Teddies have no teeth just because their mouths are sewn shut. This is not true. A Teddy who does not brush his teeth will soon have Bear's Toothache, which is likely to make him very grouchy.

TREATMENT:

Lie your Teddy down. Wrap some gauze around his head and use an ice pack to reduce any swelling. Let him sip cool berry juice through a straw — but only if he has stopped growling.

MISSING PIECES

Sooner or later, every Teddy loses an eye or an ear. If you think your Teddy has this problem, count his eyes, ears, arms, and legs. A complete Teddy will usually have two of each.

TREATMENT:

Replace Teddy's missing eye with a new button, or cut a piece of felt to make a new ear. If your Teddy cannot be fixed this easily, Mom or Dad may have to perform major surgery. For Teddy's sake, try to be brave while this is going on.

BEARLY HAIRY

Years of hugging can result in a Teddy whose hair is bearly there. This condition is almost always the sign of a well-loved bear.

TREATMENT:

You might try to glue new hair on your Teddy, but this makes a terrible mess. To cheer Teddy up, knit him a hat in his favorite color. If you've rubbed Teddy hairless, don't worry about it. Think how cool he'll be at the beach this summer.

DIRTY BEAR

This is a bear too dirty for words.
Fortunately, you can wash a Teddy without
putting him in a tub. You will need some
special supplies, however:

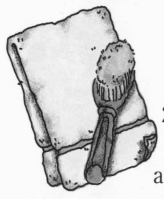

2 bowls
water
soap
2 sponges
a towel
a soft brush

TREATMENT:

Tell a grown-up that you're going to give
Teddy a bath. Then fill one of the bowls

with soapy water and the other bowl with
clean water.

Dip one sponge in the soapy water and
squeeze it out. Rub the sponge over a
small patch of Teddy's fur until the fur is
clean. Watch it — don't get soap in
Teddy's eyes!

Rinse the soapy patch using the clean water and the other sponge. Dry it using a towel. When you have cleaned Teddy all over, give his hair a gentle brushing. (Be sure to tell him how nice he looks.)

FOREIGN BEAR

Teddies come from all over the world. This can sometimes cause a language bearier between you and your Teddy. If your Teddy has two good ears but still doesn't understand a thing you say, perhaps your Teddy is a foreign bear.

TREATMENT:

See where your Teddy comes from by reading the little tag in his side. Learn a few words in Teddy's language and teach Teddy some English. Have a conversation with your bear.

No matter where your Teddy comes from, give him a big bear hug every day. Love is a language everyone understands — and it's the best remedy of all.

30

THE END